Slimy
Creatures

By Clint Twist

WATERBIRD BOOKS
Columbus, Ohio

Author: Clint Twist
Managing Editor: Ruth Hooper
Editor: Emily Hawkins
American Editors: Lindsay Mizer, Sue Diehm
Art Director: Ali Scrivens
Designer: Bill Mason
Picture Editor: Frances Vargo

Created and produced by
Andromeda Children's Books
An imprint of Pinwheel Ltd
Winchester House
259-269 Old Marylebone Road
London
NW1 5XJ. UK
www.pinwheel.co.uk

School Specialty
Children's Publishing

This edition published in 2005 by
Waterbird Books, an imprint of
School Specialty Children's Publishing,
a member of the School Specialty Family.

Library of Congress
Cataloging-in-Publication Data
is on file with the publisher.

Send all inquiries to:
School Specialty Children's Publishing
8720 Orion Place
Columbus, OH 43240-2111

ISBN 0-7696-4155-5

1 2 3 4 5 6 7 8 9 10 PIN 10 09 08 07 06 05

Printed in China.

Contents

Introduction

Some animals never have dry skin. Their skin always feels wet. But their skin is not covered with water. It is covered with a slippery substance called *slime*.

Crested Newt

Many frogs have wide mouths for catching flies and bugs.

The crested newt has two crests. One is on its back. The other is on its tail.

Year-Round Slime

The crested newt lives in ponds and streams a few months out of the year. The rest of the year, it lives on dry land. Whether in water or on land, its skin is always slimy.

Broad-Headed Tree Frog

The world's largest frog is the goliath bullfrog. It measures up to 34 inches.

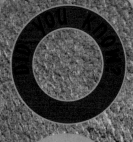

There are three types of snails—land snails, freshwater snails, and ocean snails.

Land snails have thin, fragile shells. Ocean snails have thick, tough shells.

Always Wet

The broad-headed tree frog lives on land. But its skin is always wet. A coating of slime covers it. Without slime, a frog's skin would dry out.

Snail Slime

When in danger, snails pull themselves inside their shells. They seal themselves in with a layer of dried slime.

Snails have waterproof shells.

Sticky pads on the ends of a frog's fingers help it grip things.

Garden Snail

Who Is Slimy?

Many amphibians are slimy. Amphibians include frogs, toads, and salamanders. A few other animals, like slugs and snails, are also slimy.

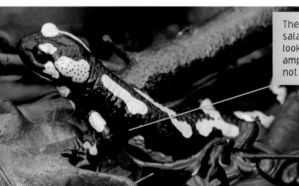

The skin of a salamander looks scaly. But amphibians do not have scales.

Fire Salamander

Salamanders

Salamanders are sometimes mistaken for lizards. The skin of a lizard is covered with small, dry scales. But the skin of a salamander is covered with wet slime.

The back legs of frogs are long and strong. This makes them good jumpers.

This tree frog has large, red eyes. They help the frog see well at night.

FASCINATING SLIMY FACTS

Many amphibians lay jelly-covered eggs in water.

The fire salamander gets its name from hiding under logs cut for firewood.

Red-Eyed Tree Frog

Amphibians

Amphibians are cold-blooded animals. They do not produce their own body heat. They rely on heat from their surroundings. Amphibians are most common in places with warm or hot, wet climates.

Striped patterns on this toad's skin help it blend in with its surroundings.

Frogs and Toads

Frogs and toads look alike, but are quite different. Frogs live mostly in water. Toads live mostly on land. Frogs usually have smooth, slimy skin. Toads usually have dry, bumpy skin.

Marbled Tree Toad

What Is Slime?

Slime is a slippery substance. It is formed in the glands of some animals. Slime consists mostly of water.

FASCINATING SLIMY FACTS •

Slime is not a very scientific word. Scientists often use the word *mucus* instead.

Human beings have slime, too! Mucus covers the linings of the nose and throat.

The cane toad's slimy poison is milky white.

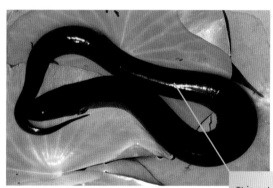

Two-Toed Amphiuma

This salamander's slime makes it look shiny.

Amphiuma Slime

The two-toed amphiuma is covered with slime. It is often mistaken for a snake, but it is a salamander.

Cane Toad

Poisonous Slime

The cane toad has leathery skin full of slime-producing glands. It also has two large glands on its neck that produce a deadly poison.

Jelly Eggs

Amphibians produce a special slime called *jelly* to make their eggs. Each egg is protected inside a small ball of clear, sticky jelly. The eggs stick together in clusters, called *spawn*.

Animals are mostly made up of water. 70 percent of the human body is water.

The cane toad has small, poisonous glands all over its skin.

Green Toads

These toads are producing strings of spawn.

How Is Slime Useful?

Slime helps animals move. It protects animals from attack. It keeps an animal's skin from drying out. Without slime, some animals couldn't live!

A Foam-Nest Frog's Nest

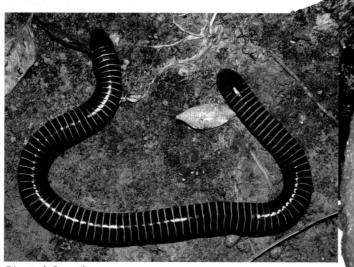

Ringed Caecilian

Slime for Movement

The ringed caecilian is an amphibian that lives underground. Its skin has a coating of slime that helps it slide through tunnels.

DID YOU KNOW?

The nest of a foam-nest frog can contain more than 1,000 eggs.

The frog's skin is kept damp by slime.

The outer layer of foam hardens to form a protective crust.

FASCINATING SLIMY FACTS •

There are more than 150 different species of caecilians.

Some slugs are more than eight inches long, longer than a pencil!

Keeping Moist

Slugs and snails are not amphibians. They are mollusks. Slime keeps their skin from drying out.

The slug does not have a hard shell for protection. It has only a patch of tougher skin behind its head.

Slime for Protection

In tropical forests, a lot of frogs live in trees. They are far from ponds or streams. Foam-nest frogs beat bubbles into their slime with their back legs. This makes a thick foam that keeps their eggs from drying out.

Tropical Slug

Does Slime Help With Breathing?

Young amphibians have gills. They use these gills to breathe. Adult amphibians breathe through lungs. They also absorb oxygen through their slimy skin.

Red-Backed Salamander

The salamander's skin allows waste gases to escape.

If the toad's skin is kept wet with slime, it can absorb small amounts of oxygen.

Skin Breathing

Most animals use lungs or gills to breathe. Amphibians, like this red-backed salamander, are different. They can also absorb oxygen through their skin!

European Toad

FASCINATING SLIMY FACTS •

The red-backed salamander lives on land and has no lungs. It breathes through its skin.

It takes days to wash a slimy salamander's slime off your hands.

This toad uses its lungs to breathe. This is how most oxygen enters its body.

Extra Slimy

The slimy salamander breathes through its wet skin. The animal gets its name from the sticky slime it produces.

Lungs, Gills, or Skin?

Breathing through the skin is not very efficient. Most amphibians rely on lungs or gills to breathe.

Slimy Salamander

This salamander's skin is dark blue or black with gold or silver spots.

Long ago, people believed that touching a toad cured warts.

Are Fish Slimy?

Fish live in water. So, most fish do not need slime to keep their skin wet. But some fish, like eels, come out of the water. Their skin is covered with slime.

Eels have thick, snake-like bodies.

European Eel

A layer of slime keeps an eel wet when it is on dry land.

Eel

Slimy Eels

Eels wiggle across land when traveling between bodies of water. Slime keeps their skin wet when they are out of the water.

Tough Travelers

Some eels travel long distances. European eels hatch from eggs in the Atlantic Ocean. Then, they leave the ocean to swim in rivers. When they are full-grown, the eels return to the ocean.

FASCINATING SLIMY FACTS ·

Young eels are often called *glass eels*. Their skin is clear, allowing their bones to show through.

European eels are believed to hatch in the Sargasso Sea. This is an area of thick seaweed in the Atlantic Ocean.

Unlike other fish, an eel has one long fin on its back.

DID YOU KNOW?

Some eels live in a river more than 30 years before returning to the ocean.

Shining Silver

Young eels are called *elvers*. They are silver in color.

Elvers

Whose Eggs Are Slimy?

Tadpoles hatch about five to ten days after the eggs are laid.

Amphibians have slimy eggs. The slime protects the eggs. When they hatch, young amphibians look different from their parents. They will slowly change into their adult form.

This male toad carries the eggs. They are kept wet by slime from its skin.

Midwife Toad

Egg Carrier

A number of amphibians lay their eggs in water. The midwife toad is different. The male carries the eggs on its back. When the eggs are ready to hatch, the male puts them in water.

FASCINATING SLIMY FACT

A male Darwin's frog keeps its eggs wet by holding them in its mouth, where they hatch.

Tadpoles

When these frog eggs hatch, the young are called *tadpoles*. Tadpoles are small, legless animals with long tails. As they grow, tadpoles start to look more like adult frogs.

Tadpoles eat the slimy jelly of their eggs.

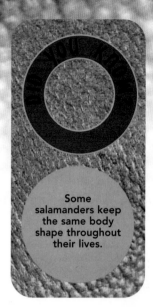

DID YOU KNOW

Some salamanders keep the same body shape throughout their lives.

This tadpole is six weeks old.

Life Cycle

Tadpoles develop lungs as they grow. They begin to come to the water's surface to breathe air. After about three months, the young frog will be ready to live on land.

Frog Eggs

Tadpole

How Do Snails Move?

Snails and slugs use slime to move. They have a long foot covered with slime. They use this to slide along slowly.

Snails have tentacles. Their eyes are on the ends of the tentacles.

Snails and slugs leave trails of slime behind them.

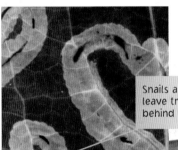

A Snail Trail

Snails and slugs have a very rough tongue called a *radula*.

Snails that live on land have lungs. Some snails live in water and have gills.

Slimy Feet

Snails and slugs have a slime-coated foot. It is almost as long as their bodies. They use this slimy foot to move.

Slimy Protection

A snail has thin, delicate skin. It can be hurt by contact with air. A coating of slime prevents air from harming the skin.

Slime protects a slug's skin.

Garden Snail

This snail's foot is flattened out to get a good hold on a stem.

The slug's foot is almost as long as its body.

Slug

Slug or Snail?

Slugs are similar to snails. But slugs do not have hard shells like snails.

FASCINATING SLIMY FACTS

The world's largest snail is the trumpet conch. Its shell is 30 inches long, almost as long as a yardstick.

The largest snail on land is the African giant snail. Its shell is 10 inches long, almost as long as a ruler.

What Is Survival Slime?

Some animals make slime to survive. This slime allows them to live in harsh climates.

Lungs and Gills?

The lungfish is an unusual fish. It has lungs and gills. It lives in bodies of water that sometimes dry up. When this happens, the lungfish burrows into the soft mud. It covers itself with slime.

This toad has special glands that produce slime.

Lungfish in Water

A coating of slime keeps the lungfish's skin wet when there is no water.

After the water is gone, the lungfish uses its lungs to breathe air. When there is water again, the lungfish comes out of the mud and breathes through its gills again.

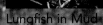

Lungfish in Mud

The desert spadefoot toad lives underground. It comes to the surface after a rainstorm.

FASCINATING SLIMY FACTS

Unlike most other fish, a lungfish has bones and muscles in its front fins.

A lungfish can live out of water for up to four years.

Desert Survivor

Amphibians are not usually found in the desert, where it is very dry. But the Australian desert toad lives there. Just like the lungfish, it digs into the ground and covers itself with slime to survive.

Desert Spadefoot Toad

DID YOU KNOW?

Toads have tough skin. One toad was found living more than 1,000 feet underground in a coal mine.

Is Slime Poisonous?

Many amphibians produce poisonous slime. This slime keeps away bugs and predators.

Strawberry poison dart frogs are not always red.

Young newts are red and brown. Adults are green or yellow with red spots.

Red Efts

Red for Danger

Young eastern newts are called *red efts*. They have a strong poison in their slime. Their bright red color is a warning to all predators that these animals are dangerous to eat.

The slime of one kind of poison dart frog is very deadly. Just touching its skin is enough to kill a person.

Deadly Weapon

Poison dart frogs make the world's deadliest slime. They live in tropical rain forests. Some native people use the slime to make poison-tipped darts for hunting.

Poison dart frogs do not hide from their predators. Predators know that their bright color means danger.

Blue Poison Dart Frog

Strawberry Poison Dart Frogs

FASCINATING SLIMY FACTS •

The skunk frog produces a slime that is not dangerous, but it smells awful.

Not all brightly colored frogs are poisonous. Some have bright colors that fool their predators.

Which Creature Is the Slimiest?

The world's slimiest creature is the hagfish. The hagfish is covered with slime. When threatened, it releases more thick slime into the surrounding water. Predators cannot swim through this slime, so they leave the hagfish alone.

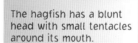

The hagfish has a blunt head with small tentacles around its mouth.

Hagfish

Meal Time

Hagfish eat dead or dying ocean creatures. A hagfish cannot bite or chew. It has no jaws. Instead, it pushes its head into a dead or dying body. This forces food into its mouth. Then, it pulls its head away. It tears off and swallows some of the food.

FASCINATING SLIMY FACTS

Hagfish live in cold waters in the deeper parts of the oceans.

Hagfish are found only in oceans.

The lamprey's mouth attaches to the side of another fish.

These sharp edges tear off flesh, but they are not actual teeth.

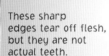

Hagfish Mouth

DID YOU KNOW?

A hagfish frees itself from its own slime by tying its body into a knot.

Only about 40 species of fish are jawless. 24,000 species have jaws.

Lamprey

Blood Sucker

The lamprey is another jawless fish with a long, eel-like body. It sucks the blood of other fish. The lamprey's mouth acts like a big suction cup. It is lined with sharp points that cut through a fish's skin.

Who Slings Slime?

Many ocean creatures use slime to survive. Sea anemones wave slime-covered tentacles to catch food. Sea cucumbers squirt long threads covered with poisonous slime to defend themselves.

DID YOU KNOW?

Clownfish live among the poisonous tentacles of sea anemones without being harmed.

A sea anemone has rows of sticky tentacles around its mouth.

Sea Cucumbers

When threatened, a sea cucumber squirts long, slimy, poison-covered threads from its bottom.

Sea Cucumber

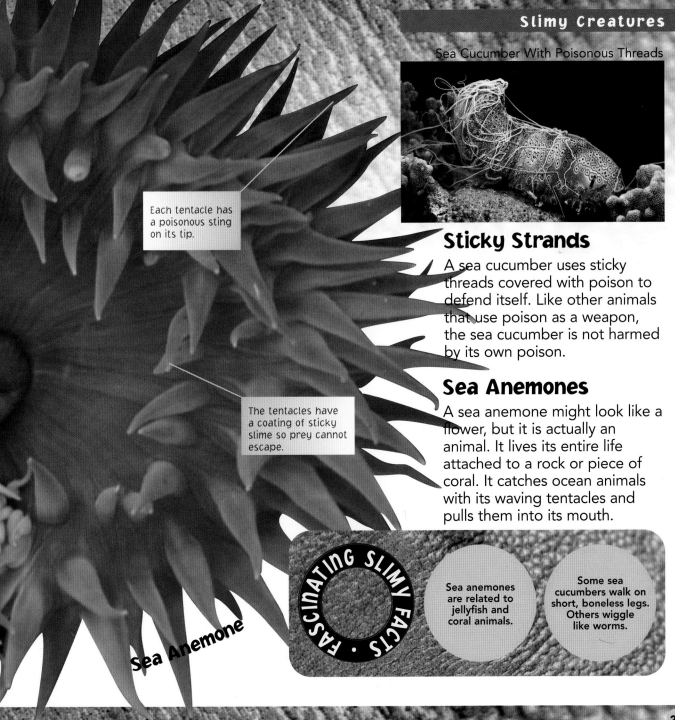

Sea Cucumber With Poisonous Threads

Each tentacle has a poisonous sting on its tip.

The tentacles have a coating of sticky slime so prey cannot escape.

Sticky Strands

A sea cucumber uses sticky threads covered with poison to defend itself. Like other animals that use poison as a weapon, the sea cucumber is not harmed by its own poison.

Sea Anemones

A sea anemone might look like a flower, but it is actually an animal. It lives its entire life attached to a rock or piece of coral. It catches ocean animals with its waving tentacles and pulls them into its mouth.

Sea Anemone

FASCINATING SLIMY FACTS

Sea anemones are related to jellyfish and coral animals.

Some sea cucumbers walk on short, boneless legs. Others wiggle like worms.

Is Slime Alive?

Stromatolites

Some slime is alive. Bacteria and amoebas are tiny, living creatures. They live together in groups called *colonies*. These colonies look like big blobs of slime.

Slime Mold

Living Slime

Stromatolites are round lumps of rock with bacteria living on their surfaces. These stromatolites are found in warm, shallow seawater.

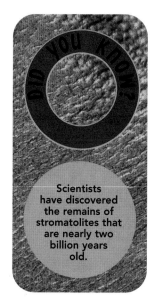

DID YOU KNOW?

Scientists have discovered the remains of stromatolites that are nearly two billion years old.

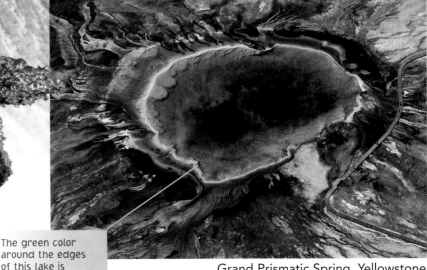

The green color around the edges of this lake is caused by floating blue-green algae.

Grand Prismatic Spring, Yellowstone

Slime Mold

A slime mold is made up of thousands of tiny creatures. These animals usually live alone in soil or dirt. But when food is scarce, they join together into a single blob of slime. They wiggle their way to a better location.

Lake Slime

Blue-green algae are bacteria that form large blobs of slime. This slime floats on the surface of ponds and lakes.

This slimy mass is made up of thousands of tiny living creatures.

FASCINATING SLIMY FACTS

Slime molds are not bacteria. The individual animals are a type of amoeba.

Some types of bacteria cause disease in humans. Most bacteria are harmless, and some are even useful to humans.

Glossary

Amoeba

A tiny living creature made up of a single cell. It can be seen only through a microscope.

Amphibian

An animal with a backbone and an internal skeleton. Many lay jelly-covered eggs in water. Most amphibians can live on land and in water and have slime-covered skin.

Bacteria

A tiny living creature made up of a single cell. It can be seen only through a microscope.

Colony

A large number of creatures of the same type living together.

Elver

A young eel, often silver in color.

Gills

The organs that some animals use to breathe underwater.

Lizard

A reptile with dry, scaly skin. Most lizards have four legs and a long tail.

Lungs

The organs that some animals use to breathe air.

Mollusk

A boneless animal mostly found in water. Slugs, snails, clams, squid, and octopuses are mollusks.

Oxygen

The invisible gas that is necessary for life.

Predator

An animal that hunts and eats other animals.

Scale

A small, hard structure that covers the skin of some animals.

Skin

The soft, stretchy material that covers the bodies of many animals that have an internal skeleton arranged around a backbone. Animal skin is usually protected by fur, feathers, scales, or slime.

Slime

The slippery substance that covers the skin of most amphibians and a few other animals.

Spawn

The eggs of animals that live in water, such as amphibians and fish.

Tadpole

A small, legless animal with a long tail. The larval stage of a frog.

Tentacle

A flexible, boneless limb used by some animals to grasp or explore their surroundings.

Picture Credits

Index